YOUR KNOWLEDGE

- We will publish your bachelor's and master's thesis, essays and papers

- Your own eBook and book - sold worldwide in all relevant shops

- Earn money with each sale

Upload your text at www.GRIN.com and publish for free

Bibliographic information published by the German National Library:

The German National Library lists this publication in the National Bibliography; detailed bibliographic data are available on the Internet at http://dnb.dnb.de .

This book is copyright material and must not be copied, reproduced, transferred, distributed, leased, licensed or publicly performed or used in any way except as specifically permitted in writing by the publishers, as allowed under the terms and conditions under which it was purchased or as strictly permitted by applicable copyright law. Any unauthorized distribution or use of this text may be a direct infringement of the author s and publisher s rights and those responsible may be liable in law accordingly.

Imprint:

Copyright © 2016 GRIN Verlag, Open Publishing GmbH
Print and binding: Books on Demand GmbH, Norderstedt Germany
ISBN: 9783668258365

This book at GRIN:

http://www.grin.com/en/e-book/335098/towards-smart-distribution-grids-a-structured-market-engineering-review

Frederik vom Scheidt

Aus der Reihe: e-fellows.net stipendiaten-wissen

e-fellows.net (Hrsg.)

Band 1855

Towards Smart Distribution Grids. A Structured Market Engineering Review

GRIN Publishing

GRIN - Your knowledge has value

Since its foundation in 1998, GRIN has specialized in publishing academic texts by students, college teachers and other academics as e-book and printed book. The website www.grin.com is an ideal platform for presenting term papers, final papers, scientific essays, dissertations and specialist books.

Visit us on the internet:

http://www.grin.com/

http://www.facebook.com/grincom

http://www.twitter.com/grin_com

Towards Smart Distribution Grids: A Structured Market Engineering Review

Seminar Thesis

Frederik vom Scheidt

At the Department of Economics and Management
Institute of Information Systems and Marketing (IISM)
Information & Market Engineering

December 07, 2015

Contents

1 **Introduction**   2

2 **Related Work**   2

3 **Smart Distribution Grids: A Market Engineering Overview**   4
    3.1 Economic and Legal Environment 4
        3.1.1 European Union (EU) Strategy 5
        3.1.2 National Strategy in Germany 5
        3.1.3 Implications for Local Markets in Distribution Grids 5
    3.2 Market Outcome 6
    3.3 Agent Behavior 7
    3.4 Market Structure 8
        3.4.1 Microstructure 8
        3.4.2 IT Infrastructure 9
        3.4.3 Business Structure 10
    3.5 Transaction Object 13
    3.6 Summary 14

4 **Conclusion and Outlook**   16

Abstract

The changes taking place in the energy sector, the transition towards smart grids and an increasing share of distributed renewable energy sources (RES) generate the need for new market designs as well as new business models on the level of distribution grids. This work applies the market engineering framework to markets in smart distribution grids. Based on this structure, the most vital aspects of local markets in smart grids are examined. First, a systematic overview of important research approaches in the respective fields is given. Second, intermediaries are seen as markets engineers in their own one-sided market. This allows to further integrate related existing industry projects into the analysis. Thus, the relevance and practicability of the research and the value of the market engineering framework for local power markets is shown.

1 Introduction

New proposals for energy market designs on both national (Bundesministerium für Wirtschaft und Energie (BMWi) 2015b) and EU level (European Commission 2015b) call for a better integration of the increasing share of RES as well as opening the market to more actors in order to utilize their flexibilities. In particular, distribution system operators (DSOs) and aggregators could leverage flexibility from consumers to avoid more costly options such as using the operating reserve and to further generate revenue from new business models. Moreover, flexibility products and services as well as other measures beneficial to the grid, and therefore beneficial to security of supply, are necessary.

In the following, this work gives a structured overview and analysis of current research approaches and real-world industry projects in Germany regarding smarter distribution grids along the elements of the market engineering framework. Moreover, all components of the market engineering framework are analyzed and illustrated by examples. In addition, future research opportunities are highlighted for each framework element.

2 Related Work

The market engineering framework (Weinhardt, Holtmann, and Neumann 2003) serves as a basis for the development of a layout for markets in distribution grids. Along the elements in the framework, this work will analyze current developments in research, politics and industry related to the design of future local markets.

According to Weinhardt, Holtmann, and Neumann (2003), market engineering is a systematic and theoretically founded approach of the analysis, design, implementation, quality assurance and further development of electronic markets and their legal framework based on an integrated view of microstructure, infrastructure and business structure.

Economic and Legal Environment   In the framework, every market is surrounded by an economic and legal environment. Amongst others, this environment consists of the federal and international laws that apply to a particular market. The external economic and legal conditions influence several parts of a market and play an especially important role in the energy sector, e.g. through subsidies and regulation. Therefore, a condensed overview of relevant energy policies

```
             Market Outcome
              (Performance)

              Agent Behavior

              Market Structure

      Micro-      IT-Infra-    Business
     structure    structure    structure

             Transaction Object
         Economic and Legal Environment
```

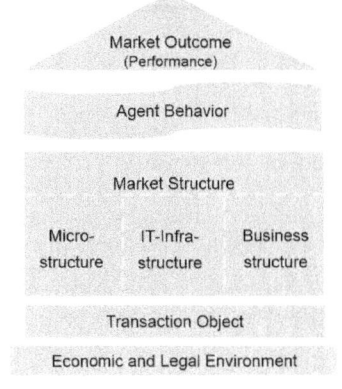

Figure 2.1: Market engineering framework after Weinhardt, Holtmann, and Neumann (2003)

currently in place in Germany and the European Union is given. Subsequently planned changes and their potential consequences on future markets are outlined.

Market Outcome The market outcome constitutes the result of a market. In order to assess a market's performance, a range of relevant criteria is discussed. Additionally, benefits of markets in general and for new local markets in distribution grids in particular are highlighted.

Agent Behavior The market structure channels the behavior of the participating agents. "Behavior connects motivation in the environment with the institution to yield decisions, and outcomes" (Smith 2006). Central to future markets, types of new flexible users that emerge and the ways in which they can be integrated into the market, are analyzed. For that purpose, different kinds of incentives are discussed. Besides gamification approaches and peer-to-peer (P2P) platforms, other current research approaches are investigated.

Market Structure According to the market engineering framework, the market structure itself consists of three pillars: the microstructure, the IT-infrastructure and the business structure.

Microstructure The market microstructure can be defined as "the study of the process and outcomes of exchanging assets under explicit trading rules" (O'Hara 1998). Here, the focus lies on designing markets that allow the short-term allocation of balancing power on the level of distribution grids, and methods by which users will interact with the market in the future.

IT-Infrastructure All facilities required in order for markets to function on a technical level form the IT-infrastructure. This work covers current technological issues in this area and further discusses their potentials.

Business Structure The business structure encompasses the business and pricing model as well as possible trading fees in auctions (Weinhardt and Gimpel 2007; Burghardt and Weinhardt 2008). Perceiving new companies in the energy market as single markets themselves allows for analysis of new business models in the context of the market engineering framework. Following Wirtz (2013), a business model is "a description of the value a company offers to one or several segments of customers and the architecture of the firm and its network of partners for creating, marketing and delivering this value and relationship capital, in order to generate profitable and sustainable revenue streams." Proposals regarding the business structure of future local markets are developed along these definitions.

Transaction Object Finally, the good traded between parties in a market is called transaction object. In general, this can be a product or a service (Clearwater 1996). As an example for future product differentiation quality of service (QoS) will be discussed.

3 Smart Distribution Grids: A Market Engineering Overview

This section elaborates on current research agendas by reviewing publications and projects for (local) markets in smart grids along the elements of the market engineering framework. Insights and possible future developments are provided for each element of the framework.

In the following, this work broadens the focus from the perspective of the market engineer to additionally highlight and incorporate the role of market intermediaries, or aggregators, as they represent an emerging entity in the current industry environment. Intermediaries can also take the role of a market engineer, where their market environment currently depicts a one-sided market, sometimes with a fixed price strategy. Nevertheless, engineering a business structure and designing appropriate transaction objects towards a market outcome still remains a valid and important task.

3.1 Economic and Legal Environment

Both on EU as well as on national level, efforts towards achieving ambitious energy targets, such as the EU 2030 targets (European Commission 2015b) or the exit from nuclear power generation (Bundesministerium für Wirtschaft und Energie (BMWi) 2015a), are driving changes to the current legal and economic environment which governs energy markets. For the case of electricity markets, a high-level overview is given in the following.

3.1.1 EU Strategy

Most recently, the EU started working on proposals for a new energy market design, which envisions a market design that should allow innovative companies to provide for the energy needs of consumers by using new technologies, paradigms, products and services (European Commission 2015b). The proposed framework should not only deliver suitable EU-wide electricity markets that allow for new incentives to integrate RES, but also to promote the coordination of energy policies as well as to ensure the security of supply. In more detail, opening the market to more actors, therefore allowing access to flexible demand and new energy service providers, e.g. aggregators, remains a priority. Moreover, establishing better flexible and integrated short-term markets to allow more players on the supply and demand side to compete with conventional generators, is encouraged.

In addition, removing obstacles for consumers represents a further item on the EU's agenda (European Commission 2015a). In particular, obstacles such as the lack of information on cost and consumption, grid charges, insufficient competition in retail markets and the absence of markets for residential energy services as well as demand response (DR) must be addressed.

3.1.2 National Strategy in Germany

In late 2015, German policy established measures that target the development of an advanced electricity market – the *electricity market 2.0* (Bundesministerium für Wirtschaft und Energie (BMWi) 2015b). In part driven by EU policy, but mainly specific to national issues, the electricity market 2.0 draft tackles issues concerning the improvement of market mechanisms, fostering the market participants' flexibility, as well as the integration into the EU's internal energy market (IEM). Of particular interest is that DSOs, faced with a growing integration of RES, are required to perform new tasks such as feeding electricity back to higher voltage levels, expanding the grid, and monitoring security of supply under new conditions. In order to ensure security of supply, the integration and coordination of markets and distribution grids is of high significance. For more details on other possible fields of action, the reader is referred to Bundesministerium für Wirtschaft und Energie (BMWi) (2015a).

3.1.3 Implications for Local Markets in Distribution Grids

Clearly, both EU and national agenda in Germany require actions to strengthen the role of DSOs. By leveraging flexibility from consumers, more costly options in expectation such as re-dispatching, balancing, or feed-in-management can be avoided. Above all, it is necessary to use flexibility services and other measures beneficial to the grid and security of supply. In the following, this work classifies current approaches and gives ideas for future opportunities along the elements of the market engineering framework.

3.2 Market Outcome

Markets are designed to achieve a desired outcome, i.e., an allocation and pricing result. The performance of a market can be measured based on the market structure and in particular the agent behavior, i.e., their preferences and actions, as well as the market outcome (Weinhardt, Holtmann, and Neumann 2003). Well-known global economic performance criteria are social welfare, i.e., the sum of all agents' payoffs for an outcome, and pareto efficiency, i.e., the state in which no agent can achieve a better solution without making at least one other agent worse off (Sandholm 1999).

Concerning the design of markets for distribution grids, market efficiency is crucial in order to ensure a continuous balance of supply and demand. Shortages on either side can result in costly emergency measures. Considering system stability, incentives of agents should be aligned with security of supply in mind to prevent market failure. Moreover, the following suggestions for outcome objectives of secondary nature represent promising, yet important goals towards the success of local markets in smart grids.

- Consumer privacy must be protected in light of the large amount of high-resolution data collected by smart meters. Suitable arrangements in the IT infrastructure can support this outcome goal.

- Market mechanisms should be efficient in terms of computational costs. Waiting times for consumers regarding feedback should be kept at a minimum and basically not perceivable whenever possible.

- In order to integrate customers into such markets, intermediaries such as aggregators are required. These in turn will only operate given viable business models. Thus, a market outcome should consider (maximization of) revenue streams not only for the market engineer but also for its participants.

These criteria can be achieved by designing the market structure and transaction object in an adequate manner.

Focusing on aggregators, the main market outcome is to allocate and in turn provide balancing power to ensure grid stability by efficiently controlling small power plants or to manage a pool of consumer batteries efficiently. For example, by connecting a small plant via Next Kraftwerke's Next Box to a virtual power plant (VPP), consumers can gain a share of revenue generated from the commercialization of balancing power by offering flexibility to the market mechanism (Kraftwerke 2015). Beegy Solar pursues a similar approach, but focuses on solar generation while providing strong incentives such as guaranteed savings (pv-magazine 2015).

3.3 Agent Behavior

Agent behavior results from the transaction object and market structure. Therefore, it is not the goal of the market engineer to influence this behavior, but instead analyze and anticipate behavior and characteristics of agents (Weinhardt, Holtmann, and Neumann 2003; Weinhardt and Gimpel 2007).

In context of the smart grid, agents, or consumers, are expected to offer their flexibility to a market or market intermediary (Albadi and El-Saadany 2008).

Strbac (2008) describes flexibility as deferring or reducing loads over time. He et al. (2013) classify consumer load types into storable, shiftable, curtailable and base load as well as self-generation. Similarly, Petersen et al. (2013) present a taxonomy for different quality levels of flexibility. By describing typical flexibility constraints, they develop the notion of high quality flexibility (buckets) which is only restricted by energy and capacity, batteries as a subset of buckets with the additional constraints of deadline and energy level, and finally bakeries with the additional constraints power consumption over time and run-time.

Current approaches suggest DR programs (Albadi and El-Saadany 2008; Palensky and Dietrich 2011) that should incentivize consumers to shift their various load types. In addition, other approaches to stimulate agent behavior might include:

- Gamification, i.e., using game design elements such as rankings in non-game contexts (Deterding et al. 2011) to support the consumers' value creation (Huotari and Hamari 2012). By stimulating consumer participation in smart grids, they are more likely to offer their preferences on flexibility to the market or market intermediaries.

- Taking up the last point on user participation, hidden markets (Seuken, Jain, and Parkes 2010) can influence and mediate user behavior with the graphical user interface of a market. Hence, they facilitate consumer participation.

- In light of the rising sharing economy (Belk 2007; Hawlitschek, Teubner, and Gimpel 2016), P2P platforms present an opportunity to communicate and share different transactions objects with close neighbors or friends. Communities can share generation capacity and increase self-consumption of their electricity. The increased purchasing power allows larger generation provisioning while at the same time decreasing grid fees (buzzn 2015).

When looking at real world examples of intermediaries, for example the strategy of employing hidden markets can be observed. Seuken, Jain, and Parkes (2010) state that "the complexities of the market must be hidden and the interaction for the user must be seamless" in cases where users participate in markets in everyday life without being experts in the field. Since this is clearly the case for a lot of potential customers of e.g., solar power plants and intelligent energy management software, it makes sense not to inform customers about the details behind the intermediaries' business models. Private owners of small power plants probably would not want to have to actively make decisions about when and how to sell their energy on the market. Instead they prefer to hand over the responsibility to a so-called aggregator who acts and trades in their favor. Existing companies putting this approach into practice are for example Next Kraftwerke, Caterva, LichtBlick and Beegy. Some aggregators go as far as positioning themselves as full-line providers which take care of the whole installation process, connection to the grid, all legal formalities and the constant monitoring and management. This minimizes efforts and increases customer participation.

3.4 Market Structure

Central to a functioning market structure are active market participants. Focusing on distribution grids, strengthening the role of DSOs in markets and enabling the participation of flexible users and intermediaries, i.e., businesses that facilitate the participation of flexible users in (new) markets, represent the main challenges (Bundesministerium für Wirtschaft und Energie (BMWi) 2015a). New transaction objects and market microstructures are emerging, while IT infrastructure considerations on privacy and security need to be addressed. In the following, details on these issues as well as flexible users are provided.

3.4.1 Microstructure

The market microstructure describes the mechanism under which resources are allocated and priced. It consists of a market's trading rules and systems, considers structural characteristics of markets and researches into the process through which prices and volumes are determined. Central elements of market microstructure are therefore the market model or auction type, the execution system, the trading mechanism and the degree of transparency (O'Hara 1998). Moreover, the form in which information is exchanged, i.e., the bidding language, is defined in the microstructure (Weinhardt, Holtmann, and Neumann 2003).

Ramchurn et al. (2011) present a decentralized mechanism to manage demand in smart grids. The mechanism manages agents through a pricing mechanism that tries to avoid peak loads. Höning and Poutré (2014) introduce a combination of an ahead market and a last-minute balancing market. Their ahead market supports both binding ahead-commitments and reserve capacity bids. Lamparter, Becher, and Fischer (2010) present a market mechanism that incentivizes agents to reveal their true preferences, therefore allowing an efficient solution for coordinating demand and supply. They note that the platform is suitable even for single local energy exchanges. Moreover, Samadi et al. (2012) propose a mechanism for demand side management (DSM) which aims at maximizing social welfare of all agents while minimizing total generation cost.

When applying the microstructure element of the framework to intermediaries (which can be viewed as markets on their own), several differences to classical markets become observable. First of all, the market mechanism corresponds to the general terms and conditions of the respective intermediary. It is these terms and conditions which basically define the rules of the trade, such as the delivery of the product and the payment period. Furthermore, usually no auction type can be specified as auctions are rarely utilized as opposed to fixed prices instead. The customers do not submit bids but rather inquire (customized) offers. As can be seen in table 3.1, some examined companies offer customized products and services with individual pricing, while others have a general fixed price product portfolio.

3.4.2 IT Infrastructure

Besides the physical grid infrastructure, IT infrastructure, or information and communication technology (ICT), is deemed a fundamental and at the same time critical component in the smart grid as it is responsible for ensuring a reliable system operation. Several issues that need to be addressed are as follows.

First, resilient cybersecurity systems that ensure data integrity, reliable data delivery and communication, authentication, confidentiality protection and monitoring as well as performance stability throughout the infrastructure are necessary. Hardware-based as well as software-based solutions, e.g., firewalls and encryption mechanisms, respectively, must ensure a reliable system operation (Moslehi and Kumar 2010). Encryption and authentication solutions (Metke and Ekl 2010; Khurana et al. 2010), approaches that extend current architectures with methods from trusted computing (Paverd, Martin, and Brown 2014) as well as complete system architectures (Moslehi and Kumar 2010) have been proposed.

Second, following the previous claim, privacy issues arise from the vast amount of collected data from smart meters. Most recently, Goel and Hong (2015) note that a breach of data privacy is among the most prevalent threats to the operation and safety of the grid. Prominent approaches include the anonymization of smart meter data. In particular, by aggregating frequently measured smart meter data, billing, account management and marketing measures must still be possible (Efthymiou and Kalogridis 2010). Other approaches include the encryption of individual measurements (Mármol et al. 2012). Moreover, designing mechanisms that enhance privacy while at the same time ensuring properties of market mechanisms such as allocative efficiency constitute an important research direction at the interface of market microstructure and IT infrastructure (Kessler, Flath, and Böhm 2015).

Third, industry standards for ICT are required to integrate a heterogeneous landscape of devices, e.g., intelligent appliances, smart meters or renewable generation, and to facilitate the real-time information flow between them in a smart grid system (Gungor et al. 2011). Moreover, technical issues such as low-latencies and limited bandwidth must be addressed. An overview of current standardization efforts is provided in Gungor et al. (2013).

Last, interfaces to the market are required to allow and encourage agent participation. On the one hand, technical interfaces, i.e., application programming interfaces (APIs), must allow easy access to markets. On the other hand, user interfaces must account for users' cognitive cost and bounded rationality when interacting with markets (Seuken, Jain, and Parkes 2010; Seuken et al. 2012).

When examining existing intermediaries (interpreted as single markets each) the importance of the IT infrastructure becomes evident. For VPPs for example, the communication between the distributed power plants plays a crucial role and mostly happens via internet connection or mobile (gsm) communication. Besides, the communication between intermediary and customer often is done completely through IT means like web portals and mobile applications. The individual characteristics of each of the surveyed companies are summarized in table 3.1 below.

3.4.3 Business Structure

Business Structure of Markets Business structure in the sense of Weinhardt, Holtmann, and Neumann (2003) concerns the charges for accessing the market, as well as fees for using the communication means (e.g., for placing bids) and for executing orders. In other words, when examining business structure, the central question is "how does the operator of a market generate revenues?".

Important revenue streams of current energy markets include fees for connectivity and trading. For example, the European Energy Exchange (EEX), charges its traders for the connection to the exchange as well as for the trading itself. Different qualities of connection - "Internet", "virtual private network (VPN)" and "Leased Line" - are offered. The trading fees consist of a fixed and a variable component, i.e. annual fees, technical fees and transaction fees (EEX 2015).

For future local markets, similar business structures are thinkable, since current models have proven their value. However, the particular characteristics of local markets have to be considered. Contrary to the existing wholesale markets, it is crucial for local markets to integrate a large number of distributed agents. This can be achieved by loosening the regulative restrictions regarding market participation. A logical proposal would therefore be to decrease one-time payments that have to be made to initially get access to the market. Instead, subscription models could be offered.

As reasoned above, intermediaries (i.e. aggregators) can be viewed as market engineers in a one-sided market. In that case the business structure of the market is synonymous with the business model of the aggregator. Therefore, after giving a short motivation for the concept, the aggregators' business models are examined in more detail.

Aggregator Concept For a successful transformation of the energy system it is necessary to meet the challenge of bottlenecks on a regional level. When integrated in an appropriate manner, end consumers offer a large potential for stabilizing local distribution grids. One way to take advantage of this potential is to establish markets on a regional level, similar to markets on a system-wide level and connecting end consumers to the markets. Assuming the majority of them would not want to act on the wholesale markets directly, small agents could authorize intermediaries to trade in their place, a concept already common in stock trading (Hillemacher et al. 2013). The aggregator would then unite the production and consumption capacities of the consumers and trade on a market in their favor. Hashmi, Hänninen, and Mäki (2011) define aggregation as "the process of linking small groups of industrial, commercial, or residential customers into a larger power unit to make them visible from the electric system point of view." According to Houwing (2010) the role of an aggregator can be taken by generation companies, energy retail companies, DSOs or integrated utilities. In addition, possible aggregators could also be new market participants like municipalities, telecommunication or IT companies or housing corporations.

Business Structure of Aggregators The increasing relevance of the aggregator concept is shown by various research done in the field. The cases of VPP operators and electric vehicle (EV) aggregators serve as examples for major fields of research and already existing real-world business models.

A VPP can be defined as a multi-fuel, multi-location and multi-owned power station (Hashmi, Hänninen, and Mäki 2011). The idea is that various distributed generation (DG) units like solar, wind, water, biogas and combined heat and power plants are connected and managed in a smart way so that they can balance out each others fluctuations. Sometimes storage facilities and dispatchable loads (DLs) are integrated into the network, too (Peik-Herfeh, Seifi, and Sheikh-El-Eslami 2013).

From the perspective of DSOs VPPs are interesting, because they can be used for load smoothing in distribution grids (Hommelberg et al. 2007). The virtual pool of networked plants can offer more predictable and reliable power to the grid. The concept allows owners of small plants to compete with large-scale power plants and generate additional revenues. As shown by Knorr et al. (2014), VPPs are not only technically capable of supplying all of Germany with renewable energy, but are also able to offer ancillary services to the grid. Therefore the fundamental prerequisites for (profitable) business models for VPPs are given.

Pandžić et al. (2013) examine the case of a VPP consisting of a wind power plant, a quick response conventional power plant and a pumped hydro storage plant. Their results demonstrate that by participating in both the day-ahead and the balancing market the coordinated cluster of generators performs (financially) better than independent generation units would. Besides, the aggregation increases the overall operational flexibility.

Another promising use case for aggregation business models is the pooling and centralized management of EVs. Ensslen et al. (2014) examine the business model of a Smart Charging Manager who aggregates the load shifting potential offered by electric vehicles and coordinates their charging process. For the reference years 2022 and 2030 the results of the simulation indicate considerable potential for "profitably operating the business model of a smart charging manager". Besides, the work shows that appropriate integration can avoid new peaks in energy consumption due to increased demand by electric mobility. Also, it explicitly mentions the possibility of the smart charging manager to help DSOs avoid critical situations in distribution grids.

As an example for vehicle to grid (V2G) services Jargstorf and Wickert (2013) analyze the business case of providing balancing power on the German market with pooled EVs. Their simulation displays comparably low revenues per EV. Therefore the authors argue "that the market for secondary reserve should not be accessed with these small units". They suggest to address other markets with easier access and lower related costs instead. Another aspect is the sheer number of EVs needed for offering reliable balancing power. Dallinger, Krampe, and Wietschel (2011) suggest a pool size of 10 000 vehicles in order to balance individual availability.

The still relatively low penetration rate of EVs hinders the profitability of business models regarding aggregated EVs. However, depending on the future development of the EV market and market access requirements they might become more relevant in the future. Through integration into a larger pool of consuming and producing units although, EVs can help stabilizing distribution grids in the near future (INEES 2012). In this context, Dauer et al. (2014) evaluate the economic potential of tariffs and coordination models for concurrent EV charging. Based on "concurrency factors", they suggest that aggregators can coordinate EV charging accordingly. More recently, Kießling et al. (2015) introduce the concept of aggregating EV flexibility and provide a functional architecture for the coordination of EV flexibility. Moreover, they highlight the need for a communication architecture based on EU standards.

A real world example for an actively operating and already profitable aggregator company is the 2009 founded, Germany based Next Kraftwerke. Aggregating over 2600 power plants – biogas, solar, wind, water, combined heat and power and emergency generators – the company has traded over 5.3 TWh on the spot and balancing market in 2015.[1] Next Kraftwerke has two major revenue streams. One is the price for the hardware component "Next Box", which customers have to install in order to be connected to the virtual power plant. This corresponds to a one-time connection fee from a market operator point of view. The other revenue source is a share of the profits generated from trading the produced energy (Energy Awards 2014).

The joint venture Beegy has a slightly different focus and business model. On the one hand, the company offers solar panels and the intelligent management and monitoring thereof for private customers while guaranteeing certain financial savings (BEEGY Solar and BEEGY Care). Moreover, Beegy integrates existing heat pumps and storage heaters and also offers batteries in a partnership with the battery storage manufacturer ads-tec (BEEGY Solar + Powerstore). On the other hand, Beegy offers services like energy management and monitoring and marketing of energy and flexibility for businesses and the housing industry. The revenue streams include the price for the installation of solar panels or batteries and the BEEGY Gateway (i.e., one-time connectivity fee) as well as a yearly fee for monitoring, savings guarantee and supplementary services (subscription model) (Beegy 2015).

In order to avoid high one-time costs that can deter smaller customers, companies like the VPP operator Caterva offer a subscription model in addition to a purchase model. In the case of Caterva, customers can rent a battery and thus

---

[1] https://www.next-kraftwerke.de/unternehmen

become a part of the VPP without having high investment costs. Caterva's experience shows that customers clearly prefer the subscription model (FAZ 2015). This supports the statement from above, that replacing one-time access fees by subscription fees can help intermediaries to attract additional customers.

3.5 Transaction Object

The transaction object is the product or service traded between parties in a market. In the case of markets available to actors on the distribution grid level, relevant transaction objects are currently limited to retailers acting and trading on electricity wholesale markets (Judith et al. 2011). In particular, while over-the-counter (OTC) products (futures) represent bilateral contracts between generators and retailers (Growitsch and Nepal 2009), the exchange model which has evolved in Germany, allows trading bid functions for individual hours and block bids for standardized block hours in so-called spot markets (Erdmann and Zweifel 2008; Ockenfels, Grimm, and Zoettl 2008). Grid operators do not interact with these markets. Due to policy requirements, changed market structures and new technological options, these goods might be redesigned and complemented by new ones (Bundesministerium für Wirtschaft und Energie (BMWi) 2015a).

The early research of Schweppe et al. (1988) suggests to differentiate products, i.e., tariffs, along temporal and spacial components. Similarly, Hayn, Bertsch, and Fichtner (2015) develop a concept for QoS level indicators for (residential) electricity tariffs, which they define as a service. Moreover, Flath et al. (2015) perform an extensive and structured analysis to derive new transaction objects. In particular, they suggest product differentiation based on different levels of security of supply, tariff components and additional use cases of power, such as for electric mobility.

In line with this research, it becomes clear that while electricity will remain a homogeneous good regarding its technical properties like voltage and frequency, a product differentiation along non-functional quality attributes of electricity services presents an emerging approach. In particular, temporal flexibility, curtailment flexibility and reliability requirements constitute promising characteristics to further raise efficiency not only on the local but global electricity market level.

Schuller et al. (2015) present a framework and design options for quality differentiated energy products and related services. They suggest that product differentiation can foster self-selection of customers and thus support activating the flexibility potential of DSM in smart grids. Sioshansi (2012) and Flath (2014) evaluate different tariffs for EVs, e.g., time of use (TOU) tariffs, and find that trade-offs between tariff complexity and efficiency are to be accounted for.

Existing intermediaries in smart grids offer various sorts of transaction objects, like hardware products for the connection and integration into the swarm, intelligent management software and a wide range of different services. Table 3.1 shows an aggregated overview of the types of offered transaction objects.

3.6 Summary

As shown before, initial solutions from the industry exist already today. The findings are summarized in table 3.1, structured according to the market engineering framework.

Due to their clear importance the two aspects of improving grid stability and generating additional revenues through marketing of energy and flexibility are chosen as representatives for evaluating market outcome. Regarding the agents, the target customers are divided into the two groups private and industry customers, besides customers owning solar or wind generation units are differentiated. In respect to the microstructure especially the availability of custom prices is of interest. When looking at the IT infrastructure of intermediaries the three most relevant categories are internet access, mobile access and the offering of a mobile application. In regard to the business models the revenue streams of the existing companies differ in particular and are therefore subdivided into one-time fee (sale), subscription model and brokerage fee. The latest is synonymous to the intermediaries keeping a share of the generated revenue. Last, the particular transaction objects are grouped into products and services.

The resulting table thus gives a structured overview of existing industry projects in regard to smart distribution grids.

3.6. Summary

Table 3.1: Overview of prominent products and services from industry (● = Fulfilled, ◐ = Not fulfilled or unknown)

	Next Kraftwerke	Beegy	LichtBlick	SchwarmEnergie	Sonnenbatterie	Tesla	Caterva
Market outcome							
Ensure grid stability through efficient allocation	●	●	●	●	●	●	●
Generate revenues through flexibility marketing	●	●	●	●	◐	◐	●
Agent behavior							
Private households	●	●	●	●	●	●	●
Industry consumers	●	●	●	●	◐	●	◐
Solar generation installed	●	●	●	●	◐	◐	●
Wind generation installed	●	●	◐	◐	◐	◐	◐
Microstructure							
Custom prices	●	●	●	●	◐	◐	◐
(IT) infrastructure							
Internet access required	◐	●	●	●	◐	◐	●
Mobile (GSM) access available	●	◐	◐	◐	●	◐	●
Provides mobile application	●	●	●	◐	●	◐	●
Business structure							
One-time sale	●	●	●	●	●	●	●
Subscription	●	●	●	●	◐	◐	●
Brokerage fee/ Shared revenue	●	●	●	◐	◐	◐	●
Transaction object							
Physical product	●	●	●	●	●	●	●
Service	●	●	●	●	◐	◐	●

Own data from 2015/11.

4 Conclusion and Outlook

This work argues that local markets in distribution grids are a promising way to cope with the challenges posed by the rapid and disruptive transformation of the energy sector. Therefore, a survey of current research is conducted and subsequently structured according to the market engineering framework. By defining intermediaries in distribution grids as one-sided markets on their own, they can be included in the analysis.

For every one of the market engineering framework's components relevant topics, research approaches and their results are presented. The main goals of research concerning market outcome are to ensure grid stability, maximize revenue for all participants, provide consumer privacy and minimize computational costs. Regarding agent behavior current research directions include gamification, hidden markets and the sharing economy. Research approaches related to the microstructure of markets cover amongst others the theoretical mechanism design and designing incentives for participants with respect to the characteristics of local markets, e.g., pricing mechanism that avoids peak loads. Looking at the IT infrastructure, important areas of research include resilient cybersecurity systems, privacy issues, industry standards for ICT and interfaces to the market. When examining the business structure of markets, it is suggested to cope with the characteristics of local markets by substituting high one-time access fees for subscription payments in order to attract smaller customers. This thesis is supported by the analysis of business models of real-world VPPs. Research has shown that they are technologically able to supply an entire country with electricity. Other results stating that VPPs can operate profitable are proven by financially successful startups like Next Kraftwerke. Business models of EV aggregators are yet to become profitable due to low penetration rates, but research shows considerable potential for future applications. In terms of future transaction objects in smart distribution grids, product differentiation, e.g., through quality of service is discussed. Research has shown that product differentiation can foster self-selection of customers and thereby support activating the flexibility potential of DSM in smart grids.

Future research opportunities regarding market engineering in smart distribution grids include the application of the structured market engineering process (Weinhardt, Holtmann, and Neumann 2003), which allows achieving specific market design goals in a systematic and structured way. Besides, it would be valuable that the approaches mentioned above are elaborated, refined and adjusted to a rapidly changing economic and political environment.

Bibliography

Albadi, Mohammed H., and Ehab F. El-Saadany. 2008. "A summary of demand response in electricity markets". *Electric Power Systems Research* 78 (11): 1989–1996. ISSN: 0378-7796. doi:10.1016/j.epsr.2008.04.002.

Beegy. 2015. "BEEGY setzt bei Gestaltung der künftigen Energiewelt auf adstec". Visited on 11/25/2015. http://business.beegy.com/beegy-setzt-bei-gestaltung-der-kuenftigen-energiewelt-auf-ads-tec/.

Belk, Russell. 2007. "Why Not Share Rather Than Own?" *The ANNALS of the American Academy of Political and Social Science* 611 (1): 126–140. ISSN: 0002-7162, 1552-3349. doi:10.1177/0002716206298483.

Bundesministerium für Wirtschaft und Energie (BMWi). 2015a. *Ein Strommarkt für die Energiewende: Ergebnispapier des Bundesministeriums für Wirtschaft und Energie (Weißbuch)*. Tech. rep. Bundesministerium für Wirtschaft und Energie (BMWi). Visited on 10/23/2015.

— . 2015b. "Informationen zum Energiekabinett am 4. November 2015". http://www.bmwi.de/BMWi/Redaktion/PDF/F/fact-sheet-zum-energiekabinett,property=pdf,bereich=bmwi2012,sprache=de,rwb=true.pdf.

Burghardt, Matthias, and Christof Weinhardt. 2008. "Nonlinear pricing of e-market transaction services". *International Journal of Electronic Business (IJEB)* 6 (1).

buzzn. 2015. "Die Kraft der Gemeinschaft". Visited on 11/25/2015. http://www.buzzn.net/.

Clearwater, Scott H. 1996. *Market-based control: A paradigm for distributed resource allocation*. World Scientific.

Dallinger, D., D. Krampe, and M. Wietschel. 2011. "Vehicle-to-grid regulation reserves based on a dynamic simulation of mobility behavior". *IEEE Transactions on Smart Grid* 2 (2): 302–313. doi:10.1109/TSG.2011.2131692.

Dauer, David, Sebastian Gottwalt, Willi Schweinfort, and Gerhard Walker. 2014. "Lademanagement für Elektrofahrzeuge am Beispiel der Netzampel". In *VDE-Kongress 2014 Smart Cities*.

Deterding, Sebastian, Dan Dixon, Rilla Khaled, and Lennart Nacke. 2011. "From Game Design Elements to Gamefulness: Defining "Gamification"". In *Proceedings of the 15th International Academic MindTrek Conference: Envisioning Future Media Environments*, 9–15. MindTrek '11. New York, NY, USA: ACM. ISBN: 978-1-4503-0816-8. doi:10.1145/2181037.2181040.

EEX, European Energy Exchange. 2015. "Connectivity: Market Access". Visited on 11/25/2015. https://www.eex.com/blob/65974/e8b0e854878e50ae201af d097495c704/membership-options-technical-access-data.pdf.

Efthymiou, Costas, and Georgios Kalogridis. 2010. "Smart Grid Privacy via Anonymization of Smart Metering Data". In *2010 First IEEE International Conference on Smart Grid Communications (SmartGridComm)*, 238–243. doi:10.1109/ SMARTGRID.2010.5622050.

Energy Awards, Ambo Media Projektbüro. 2014. "Dossier Next Kraftwerke. Energy Awards 2014: Nominiert in der Kategorie „Energie-Startup"". Visited on 11/25/2015. http://energyawards.handelsblatt.com/fileadmin/upload/ Finalisten/2014/Dossier_-_2014_-_Next_Kraftwerke.pdf.

Ensslen, Axel, Philipp Ringler, Patrick Jochem, Dogan Keles, and Wolf Fichtner. 2014. "About business model specifications of a smart charging manager to integrate electric vehicles into the German electricity market". In *14th IAEE European Conference*. Rome.

Erdmann, Georg, and Peter Zweifel. 2008. *Energieökonomik*.

European Commission. 2015a. "Communication from the Commission to the European Parliament, the Council, the European Economic and Social Committee and the Committee of the Regions - Delivering a New Deal for Energy Consumers". COM(2015) 339 final. Visited on 11/09/2015. http://eur-lex.europa.eu/legal-content/EN/TXT/?uri=CELEX:52015DC0339.

— . 2015b. "Communication from the Commission to the European Parliament, the Council, the European Economic and Social Committee and the Committee of the Regions - Launching the public consultation process on a new energy market design". COM(2015) 340 final. Visited on 11/09/2015. http: //eur-lex.europa.eu/legal-content/EN/TXT/?uri=CELEX:52015DC0340.

FAZ, Frankfurter Allgemeine Zeitung. 2015. *Ein schlaues Sparschwein für den Sonnenstrom - Caterva schließt Lithium-Akkus zum virtuellen Kraftwerk zusammen*. Visited on 11/25/2015. http://www.caterva.de/pdf/FAZ_Artikel_17032015. pdf.

Flath, Christoph M. 2014. "Evaluating Time-of-Use Design Options". In *ECIS 2014 Proceedings*.

Flath, Christoph M., Florian Salah, Alexander Schuller, and Christian Will. 2015. "Innovative Energy Product Differentiation in Smart Grids". In *ETG-Fachtagung - Von Smart Grids zu Smart Markets 2015*.

Goel, Sanjay, and Yuan Hong. 2015. "Security Challenges in Smart Grid Implementation". In *Smart Grid Security*, 1–39. SpringerBriefs in Cybersecurity. Springer London. ISBN: 978-1-4471-6662-7 978-1-4471-6663-4.

Growitsch, Christian, and Rabindra Nepal. 2009. "Efficiency of the German electricity wholesale market". *European Transactions on Electrical Power* 19 (4): 553–568. ISSN: 1546-3109. doi:10.1002/etep.324.

Gungor, Vehbi Cagri, Dilan Sahin, Taskin Kocak, Salih Ergut, Concettina Buccella, Carlo Cecati, and Gerhard P. Hancke. 2013. "A Survey on Smart Grid Potential Applications and Communication Requirements". *IEEE Transactions on Industrial Informatics* 9 (1): 28–42. ISSN: 1551-3203. doi:10.1109/TII.2012.2218253.

— . 2011. "Smart Grid Technologies: Communication Technologies and Standards". *IEEE Transactions on Industrial Informatics* 7 (4): 529–539. ISSN: 1551-3203. doi:10.1109/TII.2011.2166794.

Hashmi, M., S. Hänninen, and K. Mäki. 2011. "Survey of Smart Grid Concepts, Architectures, and Technological Demonstrations Worldwide". doi:10.1109/ISGT-LA.2011.6083192.

Hawlitschek, Florian, Timm Teubner, and Henner Gimpel. 2016. "Understanding the Sharing Economy: Drivers and Impediments for Participation in Peer-to-Peer Rental". In *Proceedings of the Forty-Ninth Annual Hawaii International Conference on System Sciences (HICSS)*.

Hayn, Marian, Valentin Bertsch, and Wolf Fichtner. 2015. "A concept for service level indicators in residential electricity tariffs with variable capacity prices". *Proceedings of the First Karlsruhe Service Summit Research Workshop - Advances in Service Research*.

He, Xian, Nico Keyaerts, Isabel Azevedo, Leonardo Meeus, Leigh Hancher, and Jean-Michel Glachant. 2013. "How to engage consumers in demand response: A contract perspective". *Utilities Policy* 27:108–122. ISSN: 0957-1787. doi:10.1016/j.jup.2013.10.001.

Hillemacher, Lutz, Kai Hufendiek, Valentin Bertsch, Holger Wiechmann, Jan Gratenau, Patrick Jochem, and Wolf Fichtner. 2013. "Ein Rollenmodell zur Einbindung der Endkunden in eine smarte Energiewelt". *Zeitschrift für Energiewirtschaft* 37 (3): 195–210.

Hommelberg, M. P. F., B. Roossien, C. J. Warmer, J. K. Kok, F. J. Kuijper, and J. W. Turkstra. 2007. *Aggregation of micro-CHPs in a virtual power plant: first trial smart power system*. Technical Report ECN-E-07-055. Energy Research Centre of the Netherlands (ECN), Gasunie Engineering, and Technology.

Höning, Nicolas, and Han La Poutré. 2014. "An electricity market with fast bidding, planning and balancing in smart grids". *Multiagent and Grid Systems* 10 (3): 137–163. doi:10.3233/MGS-140220.

Houwing, Michiel. 2010. "Smart heat and power. Utilizing the flexibility of micro cogeneration". PhD thesis, Next Generation Infrastructures Foundation.

Huotari, Kai, and Juho Hamari. 2012. "Defining Gamification: A Service Marketing Perspective". In *Proceeding of the 16th International Academic MindTrek Conference: Envision Future Media Environments*, ed. by Artur Lugmayr, Heljä Franssila, Janne Paavilainen, and Hannu Kärkkäinen, 17–22. Tampere, Finland. ISBN: 978-1-4503-1637-8. doi:10.1145/2393132.2393137.

INEES. 2012. "Intelligente Netzanbindung von Elektrofahrzeugen zur Erbringung von Systemdienstleistungen". Visited on 11/25/2015. http://www.erneuerbar-mobil.de/de/projekte/foerderung-von-vorhaben-im-bereich-der-elektromobilitaet-ab-2012/kopplung-der-elektromobilitaet-an-erneuerbare-energien-und-deren-netzintegration/projektflyer-netzintergration/flyer-inees.pdf.

Jargstorf, Johannes, and Manuel Wickert. 2013. "Offer of secondary reserve with a pool of electric vehicles on the German market". *Energy policy*: 185–195. ISSN: 0301-4215. doi:doi:10.1016/j.enpol.2013.06.088.

Judith, Daniel, Gero Meeßen, Johanna Hartog, Felix Engelsing, Frank Simonis, and Lieselotte Locher. 2011. *Sektoruntersuchung Stromerzeugung und -großhandel: Abschlussbericht gemäß § 32e GWB*. Tech. rep. Bundeskartellamt.

Kessler, Stephan, Christoph M. Flath, and Klemens Böhm. 2015. "Allocative and strategic effects of privacy enhancement in smart grids". *Information Systems* 53:170–181. ISSN: 0306-4379. doi:10.1016/j.is.2014.09.007.

Khurana, Himanshu, Mark Hadley, Ning Lu, and Deborah A. Frincke. 2010. "Smart-Grid Security Issues". *IEEE Security & Privacy* 8 (1): 81–85. ISSN: 1540-7993. doi:10.1109/MSP.2010.49.

Kießling, Andreas, David Dauer, Sebastian Gottwalt, Christian Schäfer, and Christof Weinhardt. 2015. "Flexibility Procurement for EV Charging Coordination". In *ETG Congress 2015 - Die Energiewende*.

Knorr, Kaspar, Britta Zimmermann, Dirk Kirchner, Markus Speckmann, Raphael Spieckermann, Martin Widdel, Manuela Wunderlich, Dr. Reinhard Mackensen, Dr. Kurt Rohrig, Dr. Florian Steinke, Dr. Philipp Wolfrum, Thomas Leveringhaus, Thomas Lager, Prof. Dr.-Ing. habil. Lutz Hofmann, Dirk Filzek, Tina Göbel, Bettina Kusserow, Lars Nicklaus, and Peter Ritter. 2014. *Kombikraftwerk 2 Abschlussbericht*. Fraunhofer IWES et al.

Kraftwerke, Next. 2015. "Unsere Next Box". https://www.next-kraftwerke.de/unternehmen/technologie.

Lamparter, Steffen, Silvio Becher, and Jan-Gregor Fischer. 2010. "An Agent-based Market Platform for Smart Grids". In *Proceedings of the 9th International Conference on Autonomous Agents and Multiagent Systems*, 1689–1696. International Foundation for Autonomous Agents and Multiagent Systems.

pv-magazine. 2015. "Beegy Solar will Tesla Powerwall zur lernenden Photovoltaik-Anlage anbieten". Visited on 11/25/2015. http://www.pv-magazine.de/nachrichten/details/beitrag/beegy-solar-will-tesla-powerwall-zur-lernenden-photovoltaik-anlage-anbieten_100019524/.

Mármol, Félix Gómez, Christoph Sorge, Osman Ugus, and Gregorio Martinéz Pérez. 2012. "Do not snoop my habits: preserving privacy in the smart grid". *IEEE Communications Magazine* 50 (5): 166–172. ISSN: 0163-6804. doi:10.1109/MCOM.2012.6194398.

Metke, Anthony R., and Randy L. Ekl. 2010. "Security Technology for Smart Grid Networks". *IEEE Transactions on Smart Grid* 1 (1): 99–107. ISSN: 1949-3053. doi:10.1109/TSG.2010.2046347.

Moslehi, Khrosrow, and Ranjit Kumar. 2010. "A Reliability Perspective of the Smart Grid". *IEEE Transactions on Smart Grid* 1 (1): 57–64. ISSN: 1949-3053. doi:10.1109/TSG.2010.2046346.

Ockenfels, Axel, Veronika Grimm, and Gregor Zoettl. 2008. *Electricity Market Design: The Pricing Mechanism of the Day Ahead Electricity Spot Market Auction on the EEX*. Tech. rep. Saxon Exchange Supervisory.

O'Hara, Maureen. 1998. *Market Microstructure Theory*. 304. ISBN: 978-0631207610.

Palensky, P., and D. Dietrich. 2011. "Demand Side Management: Demand Response, Intelligent Energy Systems, and Smart Loads". *IEEE Transactions on Industrial Informatics* 7 (3): 381–388. ISSN: 1551-3203. doi:10.1109/TII.2011.2158841.

Pandžić, Hrvoje, Juan M. Morales, Antonio J. Conejo, and Igor Kuzle. 2013. "Offering model for a virtual power plant based on stochastic programming". *Applied Energy* 105:282–292. doi:10.1016/j.apenergy.2012.12.077.

Paverd, Andrew, Andrew Martin, and Ian Brown. 2014. "Security and Privacy in Smart Grid Demand Response Systems". In *Smart Grid Security*, ed. by Jorge Cuellar, 1–15. Lecture Notes in Computer Science 8448. Springer International Publishing. ISBN: 978-3-319-10328-0 978-3-319-10329-7.

Peik-Herfeh, Malahat, H. Seifi, and M.K. Sheikh-El-Eslami. 2013. "Decision making of a virtual power plant under uncertainties for bidding in a day-ahead market using point estimate method". *International Journal of Electrical Power and Energy Systems* 44 (1). doi:10.1016/j.ijepes.2012.07.016.

Petersen, Mette Højgaard, Kristian Edlund, Lars Henrik Hansen, Jan Dimon Bendtsen, and Jakob Stoustrup. 2013. "A Taxonomy for Modeling Flexibility and a Computationally Efficient Algorithm for Dispatch in Smart Grids". In *American Control Conference (ACC), 2013*, ed. by Lucy Pao and Daniel Abramovitch, 1150–1156. American Automatic Control Council. ISBN: 978-1-4799-0178-4. doi:10.1109/ACC.2013.6579991.

Ramchurn, Sarvapali D, Perukrishnen Vytelingum, Alex Rogers, and Nicholas R Jennings. 2011. "Agent-Based Control for Decentralised Demand Side Management in the Smart Grid". In *The 10th International Conference on Autonomous Agents and Multiagent Systems*, 1:5–12. International Foundation for Autonomous Agents and Multiagent Systems.

Samadi, Pedram, Hamed Mohsenian-Rad, Robert Schober, and Vincent W.S. Wong. 2012. "Advanced Demand Side Management for the Future Smart Grid Using Mechanism Design". *IEEE Transactions on Smart Grid* 3 (3): 1170–1180. ISSN: 1949-3053. doi:10.1109/TSG.2012.2203341.

Sandholm, Tuomas W. 1999. "Distributed Rational Decision Making". In *Multiagent Systems: A Modern Approach to Distributed Artificial Intelligence*, ed. by Gerhard Weiss.

Schuller, Alexander, Florian Salah, Christian Will, and Christof M. Flath. 2015. "Quality of Service Product Differentiation in Smart Grids". *Proceedings of the First Karlsruhe Service Summit Research Workshop - Advances in Service Research*.

Schweppe, Fred C., Michael C. Caramanis, Richard D Tabors, and Roger E. Bohn. 1988. *Spot Pricing of Electricity*. Ed. by Thomas A. Lipo. 355. Boston/Dordrecht/London: Kluwer Academics Publishers.

Seuken, Sven, Kamal Jain, and David Christopher Parkes. 2010. "Hidden Market Design". In *Proceedings of the Twenty-Fouth AAAI Conference on Artificial Intelligence (AAAI-10)*, ed. by Maria Fox and David Poole, 1498–1503. Atlanta, Georgia: The AAAI Press. ISBN: 978-1-57735-463-5.

Seuken, Sven, David C. Parkes, Eric Horvitz, Kamal Jain, Mary Czerwinski, and Desney Tan. 2012. "Market User Interface Design". In *Proceedings of the 13th ACM Conference on Electronic Commerce*, ed. by Boi Faltings, Kevin Leyton-Brown, and Panos Ipeirotis, 898–915. ACM. ISBN: 978-1-4503-1415-2. doi:10.1145/2229012.2229080.

Sioshansi, Ramteen. 2012. "OR Forum – Modeling the Impacts of Electricity Tariffs on Plug-In Hybrid Electric Vehicle Charging, Costs, and Emissions". *Operations Research* 60 (3): 506–516.

Smith, Vernon L. 2006. "Markets, Institutions and Experiments". *Encyclopedia of Cognitive Science*.

Strbac, Goran. 2008. "Demand side management: Benefits and challenges". *Energy Policy*, Foresight Sustainable Energy Management and the Built Environment Project, 36 (12): 4419–4426. ISSN: 0301-4215. doi:10.1016/j.enpol.2008.09.030.

Weinhardt, C., C. Holtmann, and D. Neumann. 2003. "Market-Engineering". *Wirtschaftsinformatik* 45 (6): 635–640.

Weinhardt, Christof, and Henner Gimpel. 2007. "Market Engineering: An Interdisciplinary Research Challenge". In *Negotiation and Market Engineering*, ed. by Nick Jennings, Gregory Kersten, Axel Ockenfels, and Christof Weinhardt. Dagstuhl Seminar Proceedings 06461. Internationales Begegnungs- und Forschungszentrum für Informatik (IBFI), Schloss Dagstuhl, Germany.

Wirtz, Bernd W. 2013. *Business Model Management: Design - Instrumente - Erfolgsfaktoren von Geschäftsmodellen*. 3rd ed. Wiesbaden: Gabler. ISBN: 978-3-8349-4635-5.

YOUR KNOWLEDGE HAS VALUE

- We will publish your bachelor's and master's thesis, essays and papers

- Your own eBook and book - sold worldwide in all relevant shops

- Earn money with each sale

Upload your text at www.GRIN.com and publish for free